FEJ

THE HIDDEN STORY OF
EATING DISORDERS

Sarah Levete

raintree

a Capstone company — publishers for children

Raintree is an imprint of Capstone Global Library
Limited, a company incorporated in England
and Wales having its registered office at
264 Banbury Road, Oxford OX2 7DY –
Registered company number: 6695582

www.raintree.co.uk
myorders@raintree.co.uk

Produced for Raintree by Calcium
Edited by Sarah Eason and Jen Sanderson
Designed by Keith Williams
Picture research by Sarah Eason
Production by Victoria Fitzgerald
Originated by Capstone Global Library Ltd © 2016
Printed and bound in China

ISBN 978 1 4747 1636 9
19 18 17 16 15
10 9 8 7 6 5 4 3 2 1

British Library Cataloguing in Publication Data
A full catalogue record for this book is available
from the British Library.

Acknowledgements
We would like to thank the following for permission
to reproduce photographs: Dreamstime: Anpet2000
28, Barsik 31, Bjwynnyk 16, Bobsphotography
38, Featureflash 43, Grafvision 34, Hjalmeida 25,
Monkeybusinessimages 1, 27, 32, 36, Phakimata
44; Shutterstock: Featureflash 19, Maga 4, Monkey
Business Images 10, 14, 15, 22, Mr Pics 41,
Bombaert Patrick 5, Ana Blazic Pavlovic 6, 20,
Sidarta 17, Simone van den Berg 12, Angela Waye
8, Ivonne Wierink 22, MILA Zed 7.

Cover photographs reproduced with permission of:
Dreamstime: Lisavan.

Every effort has been made to contact copyright
holders of material reproduced in this book.
Any omissions will be rectified in subsequent
printings if notice is given to the publisher.

Some words are shown in bold, **like this**. You can
find out what they mean by looking in the glossary.

CONTENTS

THE TRUTH ABOUT EATING DISORDERS

Everyone needs to eat – food is fuel and nourishment for the body. Most people have favourite foods they enjoy or foods that they do not like. Eating with friends and family can be a sociable and enjoyable time. Everyone's eating patterns are different and they can vary according to changes in routine. For example, someone may eat more sugary snacks on holiday but cut them out when they return home – and it is not a big deal. However, for some people, eating is neither about nutrition nor enjoyment – food has become a way of coping with other difficult feelings.

A DIFFICULT ILLNESS

Eating disorders are complex illnesses. They can seriously harm physical health and mental well-being. Someone with an eating disorder is **obsessed** with what he or she can and cannot eat and weight and body image.

It is possible for anyone to develop an eating disorder, but no one can catch one – they are not infectious diseases. Eating disorders often start as diets, but the diet becomes out of control. The individual no longer has a healthy or **rational** attitude to food and eating.

People who suffer from eating disorders can fear eating food. They believe that even tiny amounts of food will make them gain weight.

BREAKING NEWS

>> Research in 2013 showed that about 4,610 girls aged 15–19 and 336 boys aged 15–19 develop a new eating disorder in the United Kingdom every year.

People can recover from an eating disorder if they receive the treatment and support that they need. It is important to recognize the signs of eating disorders because they can be prevented and early **diagnosis** helps recovery.

Teenagers are most likely to develop eating disorders, but children as young as six can also suffer.

This book examines what it means to have an eating disorder, why people develop eating disorders and what can be done to support their recovery.

CHAPTER ONE

DYING TO EAT

Even in the middle of summer, 14-year-old Kitty was shivering. Her hair was falling out in clumps and her breath had a sour smell. Her mother thought that she was too thin. Kitty's parents took her to see a doctor and she was diagnosed with the eating disorder **anorexia nervosa**. Kitty weighed just 32 kilograms (71 pounds) and was 1.5 metres (4 feet, 11 inches) tall. However, she did not feel thin at all.

AN OBSESSION WITH FOOD

Kitty was obsessed with meals. She needed to know in advance what was for dinner each night of the week. Exercise was also very important to her. Kitty spent hours every night doing sit-ups and push-ups in her room.

People with anorexia may check their weight several times a day, because they are terrified of becoming fat.

BREAKING NEWS

>> More and more children are being hospitalized for eating disorders each year, having starved their bodies to a point where they require serious medical care and attention.

Then, Kitty started making excuses to not eat at all. She said she had a stomach ache or was not hungry. She said she would eat later or that she had already eaten at a friend's house. One hot day, Kitty felt strange and said, "My heart feels funny." She was admitted to hospital. Her heart was weak and she was **dehydrated**. The doctors told her that she had to start eating again to get better. Eating is never simple for an anorexic person. It can be the most agonizing thing he or she can imagine doing.

Kitty is just one of millions of people who have an eating disorder. The three main disorders are anorexia nervosa, **bulimia** and **binge** eating. Some people can also suffer from a combination of eating disorders.

Eating disorders affect boys and men as well as girls and women.

>> In 2012/2013, the Health & Social Care Information Centre (HSCIC) reported that 76 per cent of hospital admissions for eating disorders were for anorexia, 5 per cent for bulimia and 19 per cent for other eating disorders.

People with anorexia nervosa (usually called just anorexia) drastically restrict their food intake in order to lose weight and weigh as little as possible. When people with anorexia look at themselves in the mirror, they do not see an accurate reflection.

People with anorexia think they look fat, even if they are shockingly underweight. Anorexia is a serious mental illness that can drastically harm the health of people who suffer from the condition. In severe cases, anorexia can even kill.

Anorexia is not about being on a diet to look slim. Sufferers become convinced they are fat when they are not.

OUT OF CONTROL

Anorexia often develops from a diet that becomes out of control. One day of cutting back on meals and watching calorie intake in order to lose weight is not anorexia. However, denying the body essential food over a few weeks can turn into anorexia. When this happens, the diet is no longer about losing a few kilograms, rather the dieter has an intense fear of becoming fat. The illness takes hold and the sufferer becomes obsessed with losing even more weight.

People who suffer from anorexia are terrified of food and often calculate the calories in every mouthful they eat. Sufferers sometimes chew their food and then spit it out, unable to bear the thought of extra calories that they think will add to their weight. They may even reject a sip of water, believing even this will add to their weight. People with anorexia pretend to eat or say they have already eaten. Sufferers often wear baggy clothes to hide their skeletal frame, so no one can see how thin they have become.

HITTING THE HEADLINES

DEADLY DISEASE

In 2012, Bethaney Wallace died from heart failure as a result of anorexia. She was just 19 years old. Bethaney, from Suffolk, had worked as a model from the age of 12. When she was 16, she caught glandular fever and lost weight. Not wanting to put the weight back on, Bethaney developed anorexia. After struggling with the illness, she sought treatment and although she was showing signs of improvement, she died in her sleep.

A person suffering from the eating disorder bulimia nervosa (usually known as bulimia) often appears to be a healthy, regular weight. To outsiders, he or she appears to be healthy and as a result, his or her eating disorder may continue, in secret, for a long time before family or friends become aware of it. Bulimics have an agonizing relationship with food. They binge on large amounts of food and then get rid of it by making themselves sick or taking **laxatives** to go to the toilet. This process of ridding the body of food is called **purging**.

People who suffer from bulimia may seem to eat normally with their family and friends, but then they secretly purge their body.

CAUSES OF BULIMIA

As with other eating disorders, there are many reasons why a person becomes bulimic. The illness often starts as a diet to lose a few kilograms. However, when the person breaks the diet or does not lose weight, he or she feels miserable and binges on large amounts of food – and then tries to get rid of it by being sick or going to the toilet. Bulimics frequently binge on cake, sweets or fatty foods – the very foods they want to cut out of their diet. The cycle of bingeing and purging can happen many times in one day. Bulimics often feel intense shame and self-loathing because of their eating disorder. Despite these emotions of self-loathing and remorse, sufferers also feel powerless to stop their destructive cycle of behaviour.

UNDERCOVER STORY

THE HIDDEN ILLNESS

Bulimia is more common than anorexia, but it is harder to spot because sufferers are often of average weight and seem to eat regular meals with family or friends. Bulimia is often a hidden illness because sufferers feel so ashamed of their problem and do not want anyone else to know about it. The secrecy and shame can make a sufferer feel even more lonely and unhappy. They turn to food as comfort, and then the cycle of bingeing and purging continues.

Many people occasionally eat too many biscuits or sweets or have an extra portion of food, and it does little harm. However, some people regularly binge and are unable to control the urge to eat large quantities of food. They then eat without feeling hunger or feeling full. They gain weight and that in turn makes them feel unhappy.

They then eat more to blot out their unhappiness. **Compulsive** eaters eat for comfort and to escape painful feelings that are difficult to face. They constantly pick at food and feel unable to stop. Binge and compulsive eaters do not eat because of physical hunger. Food becomes a **coping mechanism** to deal with other problems.

Not everyone with an eating disorder will have the exact same symptoms or share the same behaviour around food.

BREAKING NEWS

>> A paper published in 2013 in the *British Medical Journal* reported a 60 per cent increase in females with **Eating Disorders Not Otherwise Specified (EDNOS)**.

UNDERCOVER STORY

MORE ABOUT EDNOS

There are often variations in the signs and symptoms of a particular eating disorder, and not everyone who has a particular eating disorder will have the same behaviour around food. Many people suffer from EDNOS. EDNOS are eating disorders that share some, but not all, of the symptoms of bulimia or anorexia. For example, a person with an EDNOS may have disturbed eating habits, a distorted body image and a fear of gaining weight.

SECRET EATING

People who suffer from binge eating or compulsive eating disorders often eat alone because they are embarrassed about their behaviour. They withdraw from regular socializing because they feel guilty and ashamed about their eating. This isolation makes them turn to food for comfort even more.

Sufferers of these eating disorders often feel empty and inadequate.

Eating makes them feel safe and comforted, but when they are unable to stop bingeing or eating, they feel greater unhappiness with themselves. This leads to more bingeing and overeating.

People who binge or eat compulsively become overweight. Being very overweight can lead to heart problems and movement problems and puts a person at a higher risk of developing diabetes.

CHAPTER TWO

LIVING WITH AN EATING DISORDER

Leroy's mother was in despair. Her once lively and outgoing son had become withdrawn and moody, shutting his bedroom door as soon as he came home from school. He kept going to the bathroom, coming out looking pale and puffy. He complained of swollen glands and feeling tired. Leroy's parents tried to talk to him, but he shut them out, saying nothing was wrong. His mother took him to the doctor, but she could find no medical cause for his symptoms. Friends came over and asked Leroy to play football, but he would never go. He refused to go swimming, even during the hot summer holidays. Leroy's mother put it down to starting a new school and the recent breakup of her marriage.

Eating disorders can make people feel very lonely and hopeless.

BREAKING NEWS

>> Statistics reveal that 20 per cent of people suffering from anorexia will die prematurely from complications relating to the disease, including suicide and heart problems.

Parents are often desperate to get their children to eat normally and to help them to find a way out of their suffering.

NOWHERE TO HIDE

When Leroy started to vomit blood and experience terrible stomach cramps, he knew that he could no longer hide his problem. He broke down and, through his tears, told his mother that for months he had been bingeing and making himself sick, sometimes as often as seven times a day. Leroy's mother was relieved to finally know what was wrong with her son. However, she felt guilty that she had not realized what had been happening to him.

Like many people suffering from bulimia, Leroy had felt so ashamed of his condition that he refused to admit he had an eating disorder. He was caught in a terrible cycle, desperate to break the pattern of his behaviour, but unable to do so.

Bulimia and other eating disorders have a severe effect on physical well-being and mental well-being. Research shows that more people die from eating disorders than any other type of mental illness.

15

People with anorexia are so underweight and have lost so much body fat that their bodies desperately try to retain warmth by growing a covering of downy hair over the body and face. However, as the eating disorder worsens, the hair of an anorexic begins to thin and fall out and their skin looks dry and flaky.

Anorexia can make the sufferer feel very cold and tired, but the long-term physical effects are much more serious.

It is common for sufferers to feel faint and weak because they do not eat enough food to give them energy. They feel cold even on a warm day. Without key nutrients, the heart muscle is starved and begins to shrink. The body slows down. This can be extremely dangerous. As the heart slows down and blood pressure drops, heart failure is possible.

BREAKING NEWS

>> On average, it costs £8,900 a year to treat someone with an eating disorder. There have also been examples where the treatment cost more than £100,000.

THE FUTURE

The long-term effects of anorexia are serious. Being very underweight affects hormones (chemicals in the body) that are responsible for a woman's periods, so young anorexic girls may not start their periods at all. Older girls' periods may stop for a long time. This can lead to difficulties getting pregnant when they are adults.

Many people with anorexia also suffer from a bone disease called osteoporosis because they do not have enough calcium in their bodies to keep their bones healthy and strong. Calcium is found in many dairy products such as cheese and milk. Without calcium, bones become weak and break easily – even a simple fall can result in a broken bone.

Eating disorders often mask unhappiness that a sufferer is trying to blot out. Actually, their difficulties with food cause even more emotional distress.

ADDITIONAL PHYSICAL EFFECTS

When a person vomits, acid from the stomach wears away at the protective layer of enamel that covers the teeth. As a result, people with bulimia often have discoloured and rotting teeth. The acid produced by the stomach also causes a sore, burning throat, but more seriously, it can damage an organ at the back of the throat called the oesophagus. Through repeated vomiting, the oesophagus can become inflamed and infected. If the oesophagus tears and blood appears in a person's vomit, it can be life-threatening.

Overuse of laxatives can lead to constant constipation or diarrhoea and stomach pains. There is also a risk of a person becoming addicted to laxatives. If this happens, a person is unable to go to the toilet normally and may have embarrassing accidents.

Regular vomiting upsets the body's natural chemical balances and causes dehydration. This causes dizziness and can lead to irregular heartbeats and even heart failure. People with bulimia often feel tired as a result of dehydration and their faces look puffy. Blood vessels in the eyes sometimes burst from the pressure of repeated vomiting. Sufferers may have sores and blisters on their hands, which are caused by acid in their vomit irritating and burning the skin on the hands. People may also have pressure marks from their teeth on their hands, created when they make themselves sick.

People with bulimia, like those with anorexia, often lack essential nutrients. In the teenage years when the young body is developing, a lack of vital nutrients can stunt the body's growth and development. In particular, laxatives and vomiting get rid of a very important **mineral**, potassium. This crucial nutrient

*Opposite: Even celebrities who appear very confident may be hiding their unhappiness and low **self-esteem**. Bulimia can affect anyone, whatever his or her lifestyle.*

BREAKING NEWS

>> In a 2012 survey, of the people interviewed, 81 per cent had used laxatives as part of their eating disorders behaviour.

is essential for a healthy heart.

HITTING THE HEADLINES

CELEBRITY SUFFERER

Glamorous singer and celebrity Nicole Scherzinger suffered from bulimia when she was in the girl band The Pussycat Dolls. Quoted on VH1's *Behind the Music*, Nicole revealed that she had fought a decade-long battle with bulimia, "I just hated myself … I hated myself. I really was so disgusted with myself and so embarrassed. I felt so alone. I was in a group, and I never felt so alone in my life … My bulimia was my **addiction**; hurting myself was my addiction."

People with eating disorders feel ashamed and hate themselves for what they are doing. They know their eating pattern is not making them happy, but feel unable to stop. The eating disorder becomes a punishment for their behaviour.

Even though sufferers' eating may be out of control with bingeing and purging, people with eating disorders often feel this is one area of their lives over which they have control. This makes them feel safe. Food is used as a way of coping with feelings and concerns that the sufferers may not be able to express to other people or even face up to. Sufferers are also often trying to cope with depression or other anxiety problems.

People with eating disorders are tormented by their desperation to break free from the cycle of their eating pattern and their inability to do so.

GOING PUBLIC

In recent years, several high-profile celebrities such as Elton John and Lady Gaga have admitted to suffering from eating disorders, including bulimia. They hope it will help other people to feel brave enough to own up to their problem and seek help. It is important for teenagers to know that celebrities are glamorous, but they can have these big problems, too. It is important to remember how desperate and worthless any eating disorder makes a person feel, even if they look good and lead a high-profile celebrity life.

UNDERCOVER STORY

HIDDEN ILLNESSES

Eating disorders are often hidden because sufferers go to huge lengths to keep their illness secret. Anorexia is easier to diagnose than other eating disorders because a sufferer is very underweight. However, bulimia and other eating disorders are no less dangerous or psychologically damaging than anorexia. Admitting to having an eating disorder or helping someone to seek support is very important because research suggests that the earlier a person seeks support, the more likely he or she is to recover.

BREAKING NEWS

>> A People magazine telephone poll reported that 80 per cent of females surveyed said that women in films and television programmes made them feel insecure about their bodies.

Eating disorders put huge pressures on friends and family. They often feel helpless and desperate when they see a loved one battling unhappiness and a troubled relationship with food.

Sufferers often try to hide their illness, pretending to be allergic to certain foods or making an excuse about having eaten earlier.

People with anorexia go to extreme lengths to hide their food, hiding it under the table, in bags or inside their clothes. Those with bulimia and binge eaters may hide and stash food and then eat it secretly. Although family and friends may not notice the hidden food, the reality is that they do notice a loved one becoming withdrawn, unhappy and isolated.

Sufferers often avoid social situations because they are so terrified of eating in public or of missing what they consider crucial exercise.

COPING WITH EATING

Most young people enjoy chatting with friends, arranging to meet for a milkshake or ice cream, or to spend time together in the local park. These social arrangements may involve food, such as eating out or going over to a friend's house for a meal. For most people, this type of activity is a fun part of everyday life. However, for people with eating disorders, this regular activity is filled with terror. How will they avoid food?

Will they eat too much? How can they fit in extra exercise to get rid of the weight they will have gained from eating just one carrot? Will anyone notice them pretending to eat? These are just some of the thoughts likely to run through the mind of a person suffering from an eating disorder when faced with a social activity that includes eating. People who suffer from eating disorders are continually tormented by thoughts of food and eating or not eating.

UNDERCOVER STORY
EXERCISE EXCESS

It is healthy to exercise and keep fit, but people with eating disorders often exercise to extreme lengths in order to burn off any calories they have eaten. A tiny portion of food may make them feel they have to do hundreds of push-ups or jumping jacks to get rid of the calories they have eaten. Intense exercise can put a weakened heart under even more pressure. Boys with eating disorders often exercise excessively to lose weight or to improve their muscle definition.

CHAPTER THREE

WHO SUFFERS AND WHY?

Like many women, Abby's mum was always on a diet, trying to lose a few kilograms. She would buy low-calorie foods and always talked about "good" foods and "bad" foods. Abby's sister was in her university athletics team and watched her weight. Abby liked sport, but did not make any of her school teams. As she entered **puberty**, Abby began to gain some weight – a natural part of adolescent development. Very sensibly, Abby did not pay any attention to it and kept exercising moderately and eating healthily. However, one day, an unkind remark about her body shape triggered a change in Abby's life that was to have a devastating effect. Abby began to diet. She became self-conscious about her body and weight, and was constantly looking at herself in the mirror. She believed she was fat and that this meant she was a failure. She skipped meals but was then so hungry that she binged on the foods she was trying to avoid.

UNDERCOVER STORY

AGE IS IRRELEVANT

Current reports show that anyone at any age can develop an eating disorder. An eating disorder charity, Beat, has found that there have been cases of anorexia in children as young as six and in women in their 70s.

BREAKING NEWS

>> About 50 per cent of men and women trying to control their weight say that they have binged in the last month.

DIETS THAT LEAD TO EATING DISORDERS

Experts believe that dieting is the most common cause of eating disorders. What may start as a reduction in calories to lose a few kilograms can lead to an obsession with food and weight and a serious eating disorder. Some people, like Abby's mother, are able to manage diets reasonably, without them leading to eating disorders. However, for Abby, dieting led to years of an eating disorder and severe physical and psychological harm.

Any one of these young people could suffer from an eating disorder.

Adolescents are particularly vulnerable to developing eating disorders. Teenagers have a lot to cope with. Their bodies and minds are going through many changes as they mature into adulthood. A rush of hormones puts them on a roller-coaster ride of emotions.

USING FOOD TO COPE

There are many issues that affect young people, from problems at home to problems at school or with friends. Some young people cannot cope with these issues and, instead of dealing with them, try to blot out their pain in disordered eating patterns.

They are often unaware that they are using food as a way of coping. The painful truth is that an eating disorder does not get rid of other problems such as family breakup or bullying – it just adds to the unhappiness.

Some teenagers do not want to face the responsibilities and challenges of the adult world and do not feel ready for it. Girls often do not want their bodies to develop more grown-up curves and a more rounded shape – being underweight chains their body to childhood.

UNDERCOVER STORY

PUBERTY AND EATING DISORDERS

A recent research study indicated that physical changes, along with psychological changes, during puberty may be related to the development of bulimia and binge eating in young teenagers.

BREAKING NEWS

>> According to research conducted by King's College London, incidences of eating disorders vary by sex and age. Girls aged 15–19 years have the highest incidence of eating disorders (2 per 1,000).

For some young people, food becomes
a way of escaping from pressures, such as
schoolwork, that they feel unable to cope with.

Bullying takes many forms, including name-calling, unkind comments on social networking sites and excluding someone from friendship groups. Bullying can be extremely destructive – it lowers self-esteem and makes a person feel isolated and frightened. Cruel teasing about weight is a form of bullying. The danger of this type of bullying is that it can trigger a person to embark on a very restrictive diet that quickly escalates into anorexia.

Deliberately leaving someone out and making unkind comments is a form of bullying and leads to low self-esteem. This can be the trigger for an eating disorder.

BREAKING NEWS

>> According to a survey carried out by the charity Beat in 2012, out of 600 people questioned, 90 per cent said they had been bullied. Seventy-eight per cent of people with

BULLYING AND EATING DISORDERS
Teasing about weight and looks is a type of bullying. People may think the comments are harmless, but they can be devastating for the victim who turns the negative feelings towards their relationship with food. Of course, many people who experience bullying do not develop eating disorders, but for others it is the trigger that causes an agonizing and lonely disorder.

Any kind of bullying lowers victims' self-esteem and makes them feel worthless. Low self-esteem lies at the root of many eating disorders.

Whether it is verbal taunts, teasing or physical aggression, bullying has long-lasting effects. By the time the bully has stopped or moved on to another victim, the sufferer may be caught up in an eating disorder that spirals out of control.

UNDERCOVER STORY
DANGEROUS ADVICE
Information posted on some social networking sites and some websites tries to encourage people into a life of eating disorders. The sites promote eating disorders, such as anorexia, calling them lifestyle choices. They taunt people on the sites to lose more and more weight. These so-called "pro ana" sites try to promote eating disorders as a lifestyle choice, but they ignore the physical and emotional harm caused by eating disorders.

eating disorders acknowledged that bullying had led to their disorder. More than 40 per cent of respondents said they were under the age of 10 when the bullying started.

Adolescents face a lot of peer pressure and media pressure to behave and look a certain way. They begin to believe that having a slim body is all that matters to anyone. Some people with eating disorders think that if they are thinner, they will be happier. They may be a healthy weight, but when they look in the mirror, they see someone who is fat. The dissatisfaction with body image continues the unhealthy cycle of dieting and bingeing.

ATHLETES AND EATING DISORDERS

Athletes and people who take part in activities such as dance and gymnastics are particularly vulnerable to developing eating disorders. A study of runners by the University of Leeds, found that of 184 female athletes, 16 per cent had an eating disorder. Today, coaches and teachers are trained to spot signs of possible problems and to offer support where needed.

Opposite: Eating disorders are common in activities where there is relentless pressure to maintain a particular shape and weight.

HITTING THE HEADLINES
PAINFUL SUCCESS

Hollie Avil, who represented Team GB in the triathlon at the Beijing Olympics, developed an eating disorder after a comment about her weight. The weight fell off Hollie but her times were slower and she got cold quickly in the water. She also suffered stress fractures because her bones lacked calcium. Her coach realized her problem and, with a nutritionist, started to help Hollie. However, her illness resurfaced and Hollie knew that she had to retire as an athlete if she wanted to beat her illness.

BREAKING NEWS

>> During 2013, ChildLine said it received more than 10,500 calls and online enquiries from young people struggling with food and weight-related anxiety.

The charity believes this could be attributed to the increased pressure caused by social media, the growth of celebrity culture and the rise of anorexia websites.

GETTING HELP

Janine was in her mid-twenties before she admitted she suffered from an eating disorder. Until then, she had just about managed to hold down a job but hardly had a social life. Instead, she was caught up in a destructive pattern of dieting, bingeing and purging. Her weight was up and down. She had distanced herself from her family because she was trying to be independent. They also got mad at her when she would not share family meals and enjoy the occasion. Janine did not want to admit she had an eating disorder because she did not want to face the issues that had caused her to find comfort in food.

It can take a long time before someone admits to having an eating disorder and seeks help to recover.

TURNING POINT

It got to the stage where Janine could see no point to her life anymore. She was desperate to eat normally and to be happy wearing shorts and T-shirts like other people, whatever their size and shape. Yet, no matter how many promises she made to herself that today would be different, Janine was unable to stop the vicious circle of dieting, bingeing and purging on which she was caught.

Eventually, Janine broke down and confided in an old friend who knew someone else who had also suffered from an eating disorder. The friend reassured Janine that she could get better but that she needed help and support. Janine started to see a counsellor. There was no magic cure, but the counsellor helped Janine to focus on ways to feel better about herself. Her eating pattern slowly began to improve.

UNDERCOVER STORY

ENOUGH SUPPORT?

In the United Kingdom, Beat suggests that about 46 per cent of anorexia patients fully recover, 33 per cent improve but 20 per cent remain chronically ill. In those with bulimia, 45 per cent make a full recovery, 27 improve considerably but 23 per cent suffer chronically. However, according to the American Academy of Child and Adolescent Psychiatry, "With comprehensive treatment, most teenagers can be relieved of the symptoms or helped to control eating disorders."

People who suffer from eating disorders are often extremely secretive about their condition and go to great lengths to cover up their problem. As a result, the eating disorder may continue, unchecked by a medical professional, for a very long time. It is often not until family and friends finally recognize and point out that there is something wrong that a diagnosis takes place.

Sufferers are often reluctant to admit they have a problem with food, but research shows that the early treatment of eating disorders increases the speed and likelihood of recovery. The longer a person is caught in the grip of an eating disorder, the harder it can be for him or her to break free. This is why it is so important for people to recognize the key signs of an eating disorder in family or friends or even themselves.

An unhealthy focus on body weight and image is just one possible sign of bulimia.

SIGNS OF EATING DISORDERS

The signs that a person may have, or may be developing, an eating disorder include:

- Low self-esteem, constantly putting himself or herself down
- Constantly referring to weight or body shape
- Avoiding meals and making excuses about not eating
- Becoming very particular about order and tidiness, getting upset if things are not in the correct place
- Spending a lot of time in the bathroom
- Wearing baggy clothes in an attempt to disguise weight loss.

If a person displays some of these signs, it may be an indication that he or she has an eating disorder. By understanding and recognizing the signs, family members and friends of a sufferer may be able to intervene and encourage the person to seek help.

UNDERCOVER STORY

IS IT IN THE GENES?

Scientists are researching possible biological causes of eating disorders. In some individuals with eating disorders, certain chemicals in the brain that control hunger, appetite and digestion have been found to be unbalanced. Eating disorders often run in families and current research suggests that there may be a genetic link.

BREAKING NEWS

>> A recent study has found that teenagers with anorexia are usually high achievers with a tendency to be perfectionists. Often sufferers show signs of obsessive behaviour.

There is no quick fix for an eating disorder. Some people think sufferers just need to eat regular, reasonable meals to "cure" themselves. However, that is incredibly hard for someone with an eating disorder to do. A person with an eating disorder has a locked and distorted way of thinking about food. It takes specialized support to unlock it so the sufferer can learn how to eat healthily again.

Recovery takes time and involves addressing both an individual's physical and emotional needs. People have to find new ways of dealing with the stresses and challenges of their lives, without using food as a coping mechanism.

Recovery from an eating disorder can take a long time because sufferers have to face the emotional issues that they were previously blocking out with their disordered use of food.

ROAD TO RECOVERY

The first step to recovery is admitting that there is a problem. Some people receive inpatient treatment either in a hospital or in a centre that specializes in treating eating disorders. Their food intake is closely monitored to make sure their bodies are recovering. Counselling encourages sufferers to talk about their feelings and to find ways to deal with their problems. Family therapy often helps sufferers and their families to deal with issues or problems that contributed to the eating disorder. One of the most difficult decisions to make when an individual is life-threateningly underweight is whether or not to force-feed them. Parents or carers of young people are usually allowed to make that difficult decision, but the issue is more complex when doctors are treating adults. People with anorexia often do not even want a drip put into their body to rehydrate them because they fear that the fluid will make them gain weight.

UNDERCOVER STORY
IS IT ALL IN THE BRAIN?

One US study by Columbia University showed that women with bulimia had different brain activity patterns from those of women who did not have an eating disorder. Increased research into the causes and nature of eating disorders will help health professionals provide improved treatment for sufferers. People with anorexia may be helped to recover with a type of pacemaker that is inserted under the skin. The device sends electrical impulses to an area of the brain linked to appetite and mood. A study in Canada showed an improvement in the condition of the patients who were treated with the pacemaker.

CHAPTER FIVE

THE IMPORTANCE OF WELL-BEING

Beyond Stereotypes is a study commissioned by Dove in 2005. The study surveyed 3,300 girls and women between the ages of 15 and 64 in 10 countries, and discovered that 67 per cent of all women in this age group stopped certain activities because they felt unhappy about their looks.

In 2011, Condé Nast, international publisher of *Vogue* and other magazines, declared that its editors would not use models who were so thin they looked like they had eating disorders. Many people believe that the use of such thin models adds to people's feelings of dissatisfaction with their own bodies and the pressure to be "size zero", a United Kingdom size 4, starts the cycle of dieting that can lead to disordered eating patterns.

The use of ultra thin models puts pressure on girls and boys to look a certain way.

BREAKING NEWS

>> According to Girlguiding UK, 90 per cent of girls and young women believe that television and magazines focus too much on what women look like rather than what they achieve.

THE IDEAL BODY

Western society presents an image of a so-called ideal body that is far from the reality of most people. Clothes are designed for and modelled by thin shapes, putting pressure on people to be thinner. In Australia, only 22 per cent of women within a normal healthy weight range reported being happy with their weight, while 74 per cent wanted to weigh less.

Eating disorders often stem from low self-esteem, and feeling not good enough or worthless. Taking control over food (or losing control over it) is used to dull the unhappiness that the person feels. However, an eating disorder only buries the cause of the unhappiness – it does not solve it. The media has an important role in helping boys and girls to focus on their qualities and strengths as people, rather than their weight and body image.

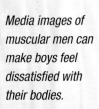

Media images of muscular men can make boys feel dissatisfied with their bodies.

People with eating disorders find it extremely difficult to judge clearly what is a reasonable amount of food for a healthy body. They no longer recognize what normal eating is. It takes time and patience for them to recover a sense of perspective. They need support to accept and understand that the body needs a balance of **carbohydrates**, fats, protein and vitamins. A reasonable amount of exercise also keeps a person fit and healthy. People with eating disorders need to relearn how to eat for health and well-being.

ON THE RISE
Eating disorders are on the rise, but so is childhood obesity, which stems from unhealthy diets and not enough exercise. Programmes to reduce obesity and promote healthy eating are extremely important because obesity puts young people at a greater risk of developing many serious illnesses such as diabetes and heart disease. It is also important not to create anxiety and worry among children about their body shape and image, which can then lead to a cycle of harmful eating disorders.

HITTING THE HEADLINES
FIGHTING CHILDHOOD OBESITY

Statistics show that the United Kingdom is the "fattest" nation in Europe. In Europe, one in three children are overweight or obese by the age of nine. To combat this problem, cooking lessons have become compulsory in primary schools, with children as young as eight years old taking part in cookery classes. There is also a new GCSE in cooking and food nutrition for older children. The government hopes that if children are taught about healthy eating options and how to cook them, they will make better food choices as children and later as adults.

A RESPONSIBILITY

Society has a responsibility to ensure that young people understand that healthy eating is about balanced, nutritious meals and not about a spiral of diets.

Celebrity chef Jamie Oliver has called on the government to improve the nutritional value of school dinners. He believes this will encourage better eating habits.

Positive self-esteem helps to prevent eating disorders and supports a person's recovery. Recovery from eating disorders is about learning to accept oneself and to nourish the body. Avoiding diets helps a person to concentrate on healthy eating rather than trying to become thin or cut out complete food groups. Nutritionists can give those with eating disorders specific advice and support about how to create a healthy and well-balanced diet.

The road to recovery from an eating disorder is a long one, with ups and downs. It is important to support those with eating disorders. Those who are ill need to realize that while there may be setbacks and disappointments in their recovery, it does not mean that they have failed.

Opposite: Many high-profile figures such as Demi Lovato are now involved in campaigns to raise young people's self-esteem and confidence about their bodies.

HITTING THE HEADLINES
RAISING SELF-ESTEEM

Disney star Demi Lovato battled with anorexia and bulimia for many years. Aware of the pressure she had felt to look a certain way, the singer teamed up with other celebrities and The Jed Foundation to promote a campaign called *Love is Louder than the Pressure to be Perfect*. This is aimed particularly at university-age girls to improve their self-esteem and recognize their qualities and strengths.

DIFFERENT BODIES

Everyone is unique and has special qualities to offer and share. There is no perfect person or perfect body shape. Everyone has flaws and it is important for people to learn to accept their flaws, without judging themselves too harshly. It is also useful to challenge media presentations of girls and women, as well as boys and men. The media implies a strong connection between being thin, using beauty products, and being happy. However, research suggests that those women who are thinner than average are not necessarily any happier than other women.

EATING DISORDERS –
THE WHOLE STORY

The truth is that eating disorders cause great physical and emotional harm. At one extreme, people can die from the many complications caused by food abuse, and their mental health and well-being also suffers dramatically. Many people have eating disorders that may not put them in hospital but still cause huge pain and unhappiness, both physical and emotional. A person may not have a diagnosis of bulimia or even anorexia, but that does not mean that their eating disorder is any less harmful or serious.

The truth is that eating disorders make people look unwell and feel terrible. Looking good and feeling good comes from strong, positive self-esteem and a healthy body.

STOPPING SUFFERING

Raising awareness of the dangers of eating disorders and ways in which to spot the signs of an eating disorder is crucial in the path to preventing these devastating conditions. By recognizing and stopping an eating disorder in its early stages, individuals and their families could be saved years of physical and mental suffering.

As more research into eating disorders and their effects is carried out by the health industry, health professionals will be better able to understand the causes and triggers of these conditions. This research will then help sufferers to receive the support they need to be able to deal with their problems and recover from their illnesses.

HITTING THE HEADLINES
THE ROAD TO RECOVERY

Writer and poet, Katie Metcalfe, struggled with anorexia from the age of 14. Her parents' marriage was collapsing and the family was moving house. To make matters worse, Katie was the only girl in her class and she felt under pressure to compete with the boys. Once she started to lose weight, instead of feeling good, she felt she had to lose more. Eventually, her weight had dropped to under 31 kilograms (68 pounds), her hair fell out and her bones ached. Katie even had a heart attack while exercising. Eventually, she was hospitalized for nine months and although she has had relapses, she has now fully recovered.

GLOSSARY

addiction condition in which the body and mind crave and depend on particular substances, such as food, drugs or alcohol

anorexia nervosa eating disorder characterized by a person deliberately restricting his or her food intake and becoming very underweight

binge rapid consumption of a large amount of food in a short amount of time

bulimia eating disorder with a bingeing-and-purging cycle

carbohydrate nutrient found in foods such as bread, pasta, rice and starchy vegetables such as potatoes

compulsive unable to stop doing something

coping mechanism way of managing something

dehydrate cause a person to lose water from his or her body

diagnosis identification of an illness or disorder by a health professional

Eating Disorders Not Otherwise Specified (EDNOS) eating disorders that share some, but not all, of the symptoms of bulimia or anorexia

genetic having to do with genes, the basic units of heredity

laxative medicine that increases bowel movements

mineral element in food that the body needs for healthy growth and development

obsessed thinking about something all the time

puberty physical and emotional changes that occur as older children develop into young adults

purging getting rid of food by vomiting or taking laxatives in order to go to the toilet

rational reasoned; not illogical

self-esteem pride in or respect for oneself

FIND OUT MORE

BOOKS

Dying to be Thin, Nikki Grahame (John Blake Publishing Ltd, 2010)

Eating Disorders and Body Image (Talk About), Caroline Warbrick (Wayland, 2012)

Eating Disorders (Emotional Health Issues), Jane Bingham (Wayland, 2012)

Keeping Healthy (Teen FAQ), Ann Kramer (Franklin Watts, 2010)

ORGANIZATIONS

Anorexia & Bulimia Care (ABC)
Helpline: 03000 11 12 13 – option 1: support line; option 2: family and friends
ABC aims to support those with anorexia, bulimia and other eating disorders as well as their families.

Beat
Helpline for over 18s: 0345 634 1414
Helpline for under 18s: 0345 634 7650
Email: fyp@b-eat.co.uk
Website: **www.b-eat.co.uk**
Beat provides helpline support and information about eating disorders and difficulties with food and weight.

NHS
The NHS Live Well pages have a lot of information on eating disorders.

Website: **www.nhs.uk/Livewell/ eatingdisorders/Pages/eating- disorders-explained.aspx**

Young Minds
Mental health charity YoungMinds can help those with eating disorders.
Website: **www.youngminds.org.uk**

INDEX